EXTRACTS FROM PELICAN BAY

"When the prison gates slam behind an inmate, he does not lose his human quality, his mind does not become closed to ideas, his intellect does not cease to feed on a free and open interchange of opinions, his yearning for self respect does not end, nor is his quest for self-realization concluded, if anything, the needs for identity and self respect are more compelling in the dehumanizing prison environment."

—*Justice Marshall; Procunier v. Martinez, (1974).*

EXTRACTS FROM PELICAN BAY

AN ANTHOLOGY OF
PRISONER POETRY,
DRAWINGS,
AND ESSAYS

EDITED BY MARILLA ARGÜELLES

FOR

THE PELICAN BAY
INFORMATION PROJECT

PANTOGRAPH PRESS
BERKELEY, CALIFORNIA
1995

Published in the United States by
Pantograph Press,
P. O. Box 9643
Berkeley, CA 94709.

Some of these writings and drawings (or versions thereof)
have appeared in
The North Coast Xpress,
The Pelican Bay Express,
The Third Force
and other periodicals.

Cover monoprint and book design by Marilla Argüelles.
Brushwork on page 9 by Anna Wolf.

Library of Congress Cataloging-in-Publication Data

Extracts From Pelican Bay
p. cm.
ISBN 1-880766-10-8 (pbk)
1. Prisoners' writing, American
I. Argüelles, Marilla, editor
II. Pelican Bay Information Project

This collection is dedicated to
Henry Gonzalez,
who has served all of his terms honorably,
with integrity and passion,
and to all those in maximum control units
who defy society's blatant and cynical contempt
by continuing to affirm decency and hope.

ACKNOWLEDGMENTS

With much appreciation to Luis Talamantez of the Pelican Bay Information Project for inspiring the vision of this collection. To Pat Shell and Ian Faircloth of Canterbury Press for realizing its merit and for donating valuable technical support. To Russel Stolins for his dedication, and to Wendy Au, Anna and Arne Wolf, who contributed to the aesthetics. And, most importantly, to my husband, Ivan, for his unwavering support.

CONTENTS

SECTION I. INSIDE THESE WALLS

SECTION 2. *MADRID v. GOMEZ*

SECTION 3. BEYOND THE GLASS

INTRODUCTION

Readers may wonder how this collection was created, if the claims made in it are valid.

My introduction to Pelican Bay State Prison occurred in the spring of 1993, when I tuned on an interview of Pacifica Radio while driving across San Francisco Bay into a sunset. The contrast between the scene I viewed, the institution's bucolic name, and the deliberate torture described was so ironic as to be chilling. To me as an artist, the prospect of spending 23 hours a day alone staring at bare, windowless white walls seemed unbearable, even without the additional threat of gassings, beatings, and deprivations.

Over the next few months, I attended meetings of the Pelican Bay Information Project, (all of whose members impressed me with their commitment and activism, and none of whom are paid), attended vigils and the civil rights trial at San Francisco's Federal Court. There I learned how Correction Guards (whose salaries start at $45,000/year for high school graduates) lobby to bolster California's leading growth industry—high-tech prisons—in which a generation of men younger than my sons are psychologically manipulated and tortured, supposedly to control murderous post-conviction impulses, but in actuality to force confessions or allegations of gang affiliation, or to dispose of those mentally ill.

Disgusted by this cruelty, and such flagrant abuse of a fundamental human right, freedom of association, I began to correspond with a talented young prisoner/poet/organizer. This led to Co-director Luis Talamantez's suggestion that I edit this anthology, a generous act on Luis' part, as he is internationally recognized both as a poet and as an artist.

Many of the entries that make up the book's first section were excerpted from letters sent to various members of the Information Project before they were graciously shared with me. The second section, "Madrid," is composed of responses to my requests for prisoners' reactions to the decision in the civil rights trial *Madrid v. Gomez*. "Beyond the Glass," the third section, contains the proposed strategies, visions, and insights of prisoners in security housing units as to how [or how not] to create better alternatives for a more just society. Its title refers to the prison's policy of forbidding "contact visits" to maximum security inmates, who are always separated from visitors by thick plexiglass barriers and so must communicate through one-way microphones.

The title, *Extracts From Pelican Bay*, is a bitter but fitting pun which refers to the prison's brutal policy of "cell extractions," during which swat teams in riot gear beat, hog-tie, and then remove individual prisoners from their cells after first gassing them with pepper spray, sometimes for as minor an infraction as refusing to return a meal tray. These poignant and stark reflections often seemed wrenched out of a prisoner's inner core.

More than twenty-five years of consumer advocacy in medical and educational arenas have inured me to bureaucracies' bungling stupidities. I was still unprepared for the extent to which deliberate neglect, lies and moral corruption undermine the Department of Corrections. Contemplating such, one ultimately becomes optimistic—surely an informed public must reject such horrific waste, if not for humanitarian concerns, then at least in venal self-interest.

Over the past year and a half's numerous exchanges, and an unforgettable site visit, I have continued to be inspired and encouraged by the integrity, courage, and profound wisdom of these men, who refuse to be defined by circumstance. I salute them today with respect.

MARILLA ARGÜELLES
BERKELEY, CALIFORNIA
JULY, 1995

SECTION I. INSIDE THESE WALLS

It is the poet's task to tear down, to destroy life's lies, to keep the senses bare, to attack. The sign of the poet's unforgiving seriousness is his rebellious laughter, which he guards with immaculate craft. That craft is constantly in need of being sharpened. Once a formal perfection has been achieved, it has then to be broken down to the bare dregs again so that the poet might escape self-parody, self-entrapment. It means a constant beginning again and again. The poet is the true democrat who has a quarrel with no one, especially the common man, the regular fellow. He remembers the guys, the tough ones, from his youth, diving from trains, plunging deep into the swamps to escape the hounds. . . . Poets are like that: rebels who take calculated chances.

WILLIAM CARLOS WILLIAMS

MISERY IS A UNIVERSAL MIGRAINE, A DULL STAIN ON THE VISION, BLOTTING OUT HOPE....

ADRIAN CARNERO
D-13629

3

THE TOMBS

In the tombs,
where the walking dead greet each other,
empty souls intermingling,
having shallow conversations with words of
hollow meaning.

In the tombs,
buried alive,
Gestapo customs replace once human kind.
Oh! Sensitivity, why have you left my soul,
abandoning me to be with moral excellence?

In the tombs,
administrative mummies wrapped
in barbaric cloths,
Eyes, a mirror of psychopathic inclinations.
Oh! Compassion, please return!

In the tombs,
I once asked the living dead,
Why have you forsaken humankind?
He answered, "It's only a job."
In the tombs. . . .

LATIF ASAD ABDULLAH
C-78059

4

A LETTER TO AZTLAN

I was questioned by silence asked to drink from the cornucopia
as if I alone possessed myth crawling from defunct cavities
first on the mysterious wings of passion and the multiple O
then on defiance and the crippling venom of youth
calling me by the nomenclature Smiley or even Uetzca
in Nahuatl the tongue of the ancient Mexica the Azteca
pulling from my open orifice syllables and consonants to
remind the tula that he (or she) is merely an extension
of Huitzilopochtli that these bronze hands belong to the sun
and the one world forever present sifting through syntax
with an uncanny eye for deliverance the franciscan codex
the sixteenth century of burning literature and history
of spreading feces to repel the lust of spanish pigs
**NOW YOU MUST DRINK FROM
THE SEVERED HORN OF POSEIDON**
So I did consuming my share of immortal confusion
and watching the beauty of death's angel circling
the destiny of my palm then falling at the pinnacle
of the pyramid of the sun to again be sacrificed
to pluck the pedals of my virgin bride with obsidian paws
screaming my name at the highest point of Teotihuacan
until occupied Aztlan—the sleeping giant—awakens (!)

ANTHONY MURILLO
E-86452

■ ■ ■ ■ ■

AND WHAT IS SOLITUDE

Today is a new day of oppression,
a day to plan tomorrow's question.
And what is solitude?

Life seems to deal justice backwards,
but yet we live, we do not go forward.
And what is solitude?

My heart pains for freedom of love,
so simple, it's like a dove from above.
And what is solitude?

As a child is stolen away from its mother's comfort,
behind these walls of degradation
does time fall short.
And what is solitude?

JAMES E. HARDESTY, JR.
D-41492

6

■ ■ ■ ■ ■

SILENT SCREAMS IN THE NIGHT

So many nights
I've listened to horrifying sounds around me,
screams in the night.

I've heard the cries for help,
the yowls of torment,
the muffled yelp,
the screams I've heard,
screams from tortured souls screeching like an exotic bird.

Screams of pain,
Screams of loneliness and anger,
Screams of the insane
Screams in the night,
Screams of fright.

Ah, yes,
this is the house of pain where I'm forced to remain.

Where many of the keepers should be the kept,
where you lose so much,
where Death is always a threat,
where Freedom is a rumor.

Happiness is a playground in your mind,
and Justice, the rich man's whore,
screams in the night.

LUIS V. RODRIGUEZ
C-33000

7

■ ■ ■ ■ ■

LOST LIVES AT PELICAN BAY S.H.U.

Lost bodies filled with aches and pains as Pelican Bay Security Housing Unit slowly drives them insane. It's a shame one must endure such uncivilized strain for Pelican Bay's vicious games. As we walk down dark halls of endless screams, gray walls are the only scene. Friendly faces are hard to see when locked up under lock and key.

Put away in California's farthest hills, only those who have been and are here know how it truly feels. Letters and pictures don't do the loved ones justice—each morning pictures must be cleansed of dust.

So hear what I say, I'm just one in a thousand here today! Living in Pelican Bay SHU is not a game. It has no fame. All it is, is heartbreak, death and pain—nothing less. This, my brothers and sisters is their human test! (But would they ever confess!)

Remember these words I've written. Like the sounds of a clock, every tick and tock brings me closer to the day I will walk. So have fear, because the next person in this cell might be some one you hold dear. When your eyes are filled with tears you will know who you truly fear. You'll say it's not fair, and at that time, brothers and sisters, you'll know C.D.C. truly don't care!

ROLANDO SANCHEZ
D-55754

PAINFUL TO THE
INTERIOR SENSES, A
FEELING OF SELF
ENCLOSURE INSIDE
MANY RAGGED
FENCES.

DORTELL WILLIAMS
H-45771

THE OATH OF THE PUPPETEER

We are gathered here today to witness the silent oath of California's Department of Corrections, CDC, the Puppeteer.

Do you, CDC, solemnly swear to maintain constant control of strings that hold the lives of prisoners as your puppets?

I do. (Heh . . . Heh . . . Heh . . .).

How will you accomplish this?

I will offer very few programs and work assignments to create boredom.

I will take away family visiting.

I will ruin prisoner family relationships.

I will place enemy prisoners on tiers and yards together.

I will bury as many prisoners as possible in the SHU, until they parole, die, snitch . . . or go crazy.

I will tell the public and judges these prisoners are dangerous, the "worst of the worst."

I will tell the public we need more prisons.

I will shoot and kill a prisoner once in a while for effect.

I will not listen to prisoners' talks of peace, but turn them away instead.

I will make Pelican Bay the best prison for officers to earn overtime pay on created state emergencies.

I will devastate jail house lawyers.

I will support and encourage laws to keep prisoners in prison as long as possible.

I will create jobs for my husbands, wives, uncles, aunts, nieces, nephews and inlaws, etc. . . .

I will remind Governor Wilson we contributed nearly a million dollars to his campaign.

I will shout at Governor Wilson if he gives no pay increase.

I will create the largest organized family in the world.

I will give California more prisons than anywhere in the world.

How will you hide these acts and practices from the public, Mr. CDC?

In any way I can (Heh . . . Heh . . . Heh . . .).

STEVE M. CASTILLO
D-89028

Pelican Bay is the end of the line.

In
the
dark ages
a convict was
thrown in a dungeon or hole,
chained to the wall for days on end
to see just how much he could stand.
Now in the 90s the object's the same,
the only difference is the name,
Security Housing Unit
["SHU"].

◆

LOUIE LOPEZ
E-78627

12

MY NAME IS LEGION

Within my early temple
there's a crowd;
There's one of us that's
humble, one that's proud.
There's one that's
brokenhearted for his sins,
There's one unrepentant
that sits and grins.
There's one that loves his
neighbor as himself,
and one that cares for
naught but fame and self.
From much corroding
care I should be free,
If I could once determine
which is me.

JAMES PORRAS
C-47703

13

CONCEPTION

Art is a conception of sensuality.
Prison is a conception of ugliness.

Grayness in the walls and the clothing,
and even in the food.
And a grayness of the soul, dismal,
gloomy.

No bright colors there, no music.
No real laughter, no song.
No beauty anywhere.

Just hard gray ugliness that seeps in, and
presses all around you
from the morning till night.

Prison is a conception of ugliness.
Art is a conception of sensuality.

JAMES STEWART
E-46397

14

A cubicle with no view
inside these cubicles with no view
is where I live my days and nights
locked in a cage that offers little
insight into lives.

Through a perforated cell front
I stare into the vastness of this insane abyss
that defies balance and logic
but I can nowhere find the child I was
when I first entered this mortared
world of penitence,
                        of time suspended.

All that remains from the rubble of my past
is my Self.

With no future nor chance
to extricate myself from this dire and
dismal fate of a life sentence
served in a cubicle with
no view to the world
And all that I ever was!

MARCOS EDUARDO VIGIL
C-36354

15

∎ ∎ ∎ ∎ ∎

EXCERPT FROM CHICANO TRAGEDY

I wonder if the barrios still stand, or if they, too, have perished from the face of the earth like their children, the forsaken sixty percenters who live only in memory, their names scrawled across some picket fence like indelible symbols of their former selves—true barrio warriors who carried the banners of their calling with heads held high, backs ever to the wind, stolen from us long ago.

We ran about the streets like nocturnal creatures of the night, seeking our fame and fortune in an impoverished landscape. That landscape offered us little hope and gave us only bumps and bruises that our broken and bullet-riddled bodies bore from the countless street wars fought throughout the barrios of Califas—Chicanos chasing down Chicanos as if they were raptors in some primordial hunt for wild game.

MARCOS EDUARDO VIGIL
C-36354

PELICAN BAY
STATE PRISON
IS A PURE INJECTION
OF PSYCHOLOGICAL
AND PHYSICAL
TORTURE,
SOCIAL DEPRIVATION,
AND MORAL
OBSCENITY
TRAVELING THROUGH
THE VEINS OF
HUMANITY,
AN OVERDOSE OF
INSANITY,
MANIFESTATION OF
A SOCIETY PERFORMING
ORAL COPULATION
ON THE ERECTED
INJUSTICE OF FASCISM.

ABDUL SHAKUR
S/N J. HARVEY
C-48884

WHAT DO YOU SEE ?
decaying society torn apart,
riddled in bullets, drugs,
deaths, self destruction, broken families
(prisons without walls or/and bars).

WHAT DO YOU SEE?—courtrooms
full of angry youths, both men and women,
victims of a decaying society.

WHAT DO YOU SEE?—ourselves thrown into
California's prisons to be warehoused, never confronting the real
problem—how we allowed ourselves to be exploited, manipulated.

YES, WE SEE WHAT YOU SEE—YOURSELF.
Yes, we are from you. We call upon our communities to take a
stand. Organize, join forces with outside entities. Demand that we as
prisoners be provided with the proper and correct tools to uplift us
culturally, historically, educationally,
to eradicate this internal illness we have taken on.

DO YOU SEE WHAT WE SEE? THEN LET US CHANGE IT TOGETHER FROM WITHIN.

PAUL REDD
B-72683

18

THREE

Simple moments, to thus we share and relinquish;
Yet the death of a friendship is heavenly missed.
The beginning of two beings becoming closeness to one
can bring a silent and gentle inspiration,
 it's the part of loving someone.
We look at all the smiles, and we still drown in each tear,
and as sleep grasps our mentalities, restlessly we still fear. . . .
Who could ever consider or even perform such a thought!
"Murder, Rage, and Pain!"
It's all our society has ever taught.
So we dream of inner feelings that may bring to us great joy,
but reminded of our hate. . . .
A glimpse of selfishness, is this mankind's condemned fate?
Who justifies the Right and sets such demands—to put to
death life's precious gifts, to destroy all God's beauties of
water and land?
Must we suffer and continue to die?
Do we in ignorant misery just give up, shudder, and cry?
Do we forget yesterday, the guilts, and all its pain,
or do we neglect all the children killed,
their souls restlessly lost in vain?
"Question yourself, only you can make it right!"
We wonder and express confusement,
how drastic and terrible can this sad vision truly be!
Look out your window . . . she was only three.

SHAWN WISHTEYAH
E-99294

SHAWN WISHTEYAH
E-99294

20

We both

been kicking around the universe

for some time now,

alone,

and doing all right.

But somewhere in the back of our hearts

was a tugging—

not a perpetual longing,

but some subtle gnawing—

that we might be better

together

than alone apart.

JIMMIE SAIZ
H-46787

IN THIS PLACE

Within
the dark bowels
of this prison, the walls rise
twenty feet, blocking out the sun.
Creating a cement and steel tomb for the living,
whose life of hell is never done. No quiet or solitude,
yet always alone, trying to keep sanity in place—a hard
task for any person who has to wear a mask to cover
all emotion. Within the dark bowels of this prison,
the animal instinct needed to survive exists
in each prisoner's heart and mind,
as he continues his lone fight
to stay alive.

ROBERT C. FUENTES
C-88749

DEMENTIA PRAECOX

in the abdominal region of my toltec civilization
nietzsche's superman spawns the universe of resentment
and shatters the fruit of manifest destiny
while the dismembered limbs of my youth seek asylum
in the deepest pores of your sacred continent
I survive on a surplus of anti–defiance
but somewhere in nowhere my existence is unknown
I glide on the putrid wings of eternal chaos
and wear the rotted flesh of my ancestors
to represent the emergence of a separate being
IS IT POSSIBLE TO EXIST
IN THE REALM OF NONEXISTENCE?
I've explored this question in detail even in detox
and the inevitable conclusion is dementia praecox
but not on behalf of my twenty–two clients

ANTHONY MURILLO
E-86452

SECTION II. *MADRID* v. *GOMEZ*

Life in the United States is alienated and oppressive not because advanced technology or human nature are innately evil, but because our institutions and consciousnesses have evolved historically, largely in "entwinement," each finally coming into accord with the requisites of reproducing society's core characteristics, and not with any more humane dictates. Our society is an alienated place to live because its main features are concerned not with human fulfillment but with the reproduction of the oppressive defining characteristics. We get law, schooling, technology, jobs, and even art, not to further human capabilities but rather to reproduce racism, sexism, hierarchy, and classism. . . .

[When] police help people, it's . . . a by-product of their real purpose of protecting wealth and power; notice what happens when the interests of wealth and power clearly conflict with those of human development. Even the medical system runs by rewarding wealth and power and reinforcing racial and sexual divisions; it serves health only as a means to these ends and not nearly as well nor as humanely as it might under a different social arrangement. Non-elite schools are aimed at preparing people to endure boredom, to take orders, and to know precisely what they need to know to fit into awaiting social roles; they educate only as much as societal reproduction requires. Similarly, by their organization, design, and technology our jobs tend to reproduce all those personality traits essential for the system's reproduction and to smother the rest. These phenomena are not often calculated and maliciously planned. Rather, they are usually an outcome of the way social changes in our system finally percolate into accord with our society's core characteristics.

– Michael Albert and Robin Hahnel, *UNORTHODOX MARXISM, (THE HUMAN CENTER), PAGE 180.*

THE *MADRID V. GOMEZ* DECISION

Pelican Bay State Prison opened in the fall of 1989. The cruel conditions in the prison and its notorious Security Housing Unit forced the prisoners to begin a jailhouse legal effort demanding that the Northern California District Federal Court intervene to stop the abuse. By the end of 1991 prisoners had filed more than 250 meritorious cases about Pelican Bay in the Northern District. The presiding Judge, Thelton Henderson, was so impressed by the prisoners' legal assault that he recruited a large law firm to summarize all of the claims into a class action law suit. The class action civil rights suit, *Madrid v. Gomez* was tried by Judge Henderson in his San Francisco courtroom during the fall and winter of 1993. The final papers were filed in January, 1994. The Judge made his ruling on January 10, 1995.

After one year of deliberation Federal Judge Thelton Henderson ordered an end to "the pattern of needless and officially sanctioned brutality" at Pelican Bay State Prison. His strongly worded 344 page decision ruled that California's Department of Corrections violated the Eighth Amendment of the U.S. Constitution by allowing and, in fact, encouraging guards to use "grossly excessive" force. The Judge also found medical and psychiatric care deliberately and maliciously neglectful, causing loss of life, disability, and severe mental harm. As relief the Court appointed a Special Master to negotiate between the CDoC and prisoners' lawyers in the development of a plan to solve the cited violations.

This landmark decision is a moral victory for prisoners at Pelican Bay and nationwide. PBSP and its 1,056 bed Security Housing Unit (SHU) was designed as the high-tech, electronic Control Unit Prison model for the nation. The Judge fell short of closing the windowless, above ground bunker–like SHU, but he demanded significant changes in policies and practices at Pelican Bay.

However, the CDoC has a history of not implementing court orders intended to relieve prisoners. It is presently in contempt of a 1990 Consent Decree ordered by Judge Henderson's colleague in the Northern District's Federal Court concerning medical and psychiatric care for prisoners at the Correctional Medical Facility at Vacaville.

While acknowledging CDoC's pattern of obstructionism, Judge Henderson offered no special orders or techniques to insure adequate compliance. As a result, the first plans offered by the CDoC in *Madrid* negotiations were attempts to avoid compliance through foot–dragging or outright refusal.

EXCESSIVE FORCE

This civil rights trial revealed routine beating of prisoners after restraint in chains, backroom beatings, and "criminally reckless" violent behavior by guards, especially in the SHU. A dozen incidents were cited as examples of severe brutality wherein reports by guards were obviously falsified and accepted by administrative supervisors without comment. In no incident was the security of the institution threatened. The Court observed that cell extractions of prisoners by helmeted, shielded, armed guards, the use of outdoor cages and hog-tying were used to inflict pain, rather than for institutional security.

Since the trial closed in January, 1994, independent investigations by the Pelican Bay Information Project find cell extractions continuing one to three times a week, new ways of caging, hog-tie chaining and even suit-casing (being carried by chains with ankles attached to wrists tied behind the back).

The Judge's only criticism of the use of lethal force that resulted in the death of four and injury of other prisoners was to declare the policy on gun use "poor and not well implemented." He failed to take into account that California prison guards have shot and killed 27 prisoners in the last five years, while during the same period seven prisoners have been killed by guards in all other 49 states combined.

MEDICAL AND PSYCHIATRIC CARE

The Court agreed with the prisoners' medical expert, Armand Start, MD, who found "the entire system grossly inadequate and unsatisfactory in meeting the health care needs of the inmate population. It is deplorably inadequate." Staff training is nonexistent. There are no crisis drills and no emergency care training or suicide prevention program. Records are disorganized, incomplete and contradictory. Supervision is seriously deficient.

Medical and psychiatric charts revealed a flippant attitude about prisoner pain and suffering. Medical Technical Assistants (MTAs) have one year of training after high school as Licensed Vocational Nurses. MTAs are actually custody staff who perform complex tasks of diagnosis and treatment far beyond their skill. In one case, a man died of a brain hemorrhage six hours after being told by the MTA that he "was faking it."

Judge Henderson states that CDoC "created a prison which would necessarily and inevitably result in an extensive demand for mental health services, yet they scarcely bothered to furnish mental health services at all." CDoC transferred hundreds of psychiatric patients with histories of alleged violent or assaultive behavior to the Pelican Bay SHU, but failed to even hire a regular staff psychiatrist for two and a half years.

The Court's decision clearly outlines deficiencies and attributes them to deliberately poor planning, substandard training and review, and inadequate and neglectful program development. Yet it fails to recognize that ordinary daily custody routines and the physical environment of the SHU, itself, interferes with delivery of care, and prejudices people into the attitude and behavior it has condemned.

SEGREGATION OF PRISON GANG AFFILIATES

Eighty-seven percent of SHU prisoners are brown or black. More than half are kept on charges that they are members or affiliates of prison gangs, which CDoC defines as "any formal or informal group of three or more which has a common name or symbol, whose members have engaged in two or more activities or unlawful acts or acts of misconduct classified as serious."

More than 800 prisoners have been gang labeled by the investigative and classification committees using as evidence names listed in address books, tattoos, pictures of men taken on the prison yard, and ambiguous testimony by other prisoners.

Once labelled, a prisoner faces the "Snitch, Parole, or Die" policy, which states that to exit the SHU he must confess to crimes and name others, finish his sentence and parole, or die. Not only is information obtained under duress notoriously unreliable, but the subjection of prisoners to prolonged solitary confinement in order to extract information is a violation of human rights, and prohibited even under the Geneva Accords adopted for wartime combatants. The Judge left intact this "kangaroo court" classification system and the use of SHU confinement to force confessions.

SECURITY HOUSING CONDITIONS

When discussing the severe conditions of sensory deprivation and isolation in the SHU, the Court backed away from significant human rights issues when it asserted " . . . [CDoC] may emphasize idleness, deterrence, and deprivation over rehabilitation. This is not a matter for judicial review or concern unless evidence demonstrates conditions so extreme as to violate basic concepts of humanity and deprive inmates of a minimal level of life's basic needs." The Court added "there is nothing improper about lengthy or indefinite segregation for discipline or security reasons."

The Court did demand certain prisoners be excluded from the SHU because they would be harmed too severely: those prone to mental illness, including those with a prior psychiatric problems, borderline personality disorders, brain damage, mental retardation, chronic depression or impulsive personality. The Judge expressed disdain for CDoC because it ignored the exact same recommendation by its own Mental Health Services Branch before PBSP opened. He warned CDoC that sedating mentally ill inmates into a stupor fails to pass Constitutional muster. But he did not address the issue that in a separate case CDoC's entire mental health system has been ruled unconstitutional.

CONCLUSION

The Pelican Bay Information Project is convinced the only way Judge Henderson could have stopped the human rights violations at PBSP was by closing the SHU. The Judge did not order an ongoing mechanism of citizen review or oversight, and no compelling penalties were established, despite CDoC's refusal to comply with the law in this and other cases. His decision leaves intact long-term solitary confinement; racial discrimination in placing prisoners in the SHU; the notorious "Snitch, Parole or Die" policy; forced confessions about gang activity; and use of hearsay evidence in gang labelling. These practices constitute torture, and are defined as illegal by the U.S. Constitution and UN International Treaties signed by the U.S.A. All of these documents deplore the very actions the Judge allows.

JULY, 1995
PELICAN BAY INFORMATION PROJECT,
2489 MISSION STREET, # 28
SAN FRANCISCO, CALIFORNIA 94110
(415) 821-6545

■ ■ ■ ■ ■

DUE PROCESS AND THE *MADRID* HEARING

The ruling in the *Madrid v. Gomez* decision will go far to address Eighth Amendment violations if it corrects blatant use of force at Pelican Bay and establishes a mental and medical health care system that meets current standards of the Constitution. Beyond this, very little will change for the good at Pelican Bay.

It is ironic that the major thrust of the class litigation evolving into *Madrid v. Gomez* dealt with the precarious, unconstitutional conditions of confinement of prisoners serving indeterminate terms in the SHU for alleged affiliation with a prison gang. Lack of focus and understanding of the history of prison litigation in this area by prisoners' attorneys allowed prison officials to dodge this constitutional bullet, and demonstrates a major flaw in strategy and prioritizing of issues.

The history of due process violations such as those faced by SHU prisoners on indeterminate status are inscribed in various Northern District Court rulings in the long line of prison rights decisions, concluding with *Toussaint v. McCarthy VI* (9th Circuit, 1990) 926 F. 2nd 800.

Competent counsel would have first analyzed the court's rulings in these decisions, determined the best criteria for demonstrating prison officials' constitutional violations, and then devised a meaningful strategy of attack. This would have prevented prison officials from squirming beyond constitutional limits by the illegal use of confidential informants, insidious/invidious process and criteria of debriefings, and inadequate, biased committee reviews. Instead a halfhearted attack was launched, without appropriate research and evidence being gathered and presented in order to "demonstrate" constitutional violations, as opposed to merely alleging them. Competence requires knowing, and surpassing, the threshold level of evidence needed to prove a controversial issue of fact and law. Since this evidence was readily available, we must wonder why it was never adequately presented, nor vigorously argued. Until these specific issues are addressed in the courts, we will remain functioning in draconian times, claiming superficial victories in this legal war of attrition.

Although something positive came out of the *Madrid* decision, its ruling covers a small segment of what needs to be addressed in the prison litigation movement. Prisoners' rights are under attack from various fronts: "three–strikes" laws, repeal of the prisoners' bill of rights, prison construction, and the major negative influence that the CCPOA (California Correctional Peace Officers' Association) has over proposed and pending litigation dealing with the law and prisons. Those committed to the struggle of prisoners' rights must put aside petty differences in order to unify, network, and consolidate resources. Important issues must no longer be addressed through fragmented tunnel-vision. If our focus and priorities continue to be distracted by sensationalism, as opposed to being concentrated on substance, we will find ourselves continuing to live in a world of deception, waging losing battles, and claiming false victories.

Hopefully this last experience and the present political climate has proven to us (once again) that nothing can be taken for granted. While we are allowing ourselves to be "distracted," the opposition is focused and determined to reverse any gains previously made and currently pursued by prisoners.

Continuing the struggle,

C. ASKARI KWELI
S/N FLOYD NELSON
B-94350

REFLECTIONS ON THE MADRID DECISION

The conditions here in SHU are deplorable. The purpose of this place is to strip us of our humanity/manhood/capacity to be productive. In all honesty, I don't see this condition changing anytime soon. Especially in light of the recent court ruling in the *Madrid* Case.

I was a little amazed at how on the one hand, the Judge found the conditions in SHU—the isolation, lack of human/ social contact, the lack of any meaningful programs, etc.—to be indecent, but at the same time, found justification in the continued existence of this madness, and by hiding behind the institutional security, justified the continued subjecting of certain prisoners to long term confinement ("indeterminate terms") by essentially taking the position that "some people can handle it, while others can't!" A ruling like this has nothing to do with right, wrong, or principle.

I don't think that many of the prisoners serving indeterminate terms believed the court would order the release of any of us to the general prison population. But at least some of us had hoped the court would consider alternatives, such as the reopening of management control units that existed at San Quentin in the latter 1970–1980s. The purpose of these units was to house prisoners, supposedly prison group members, who had not done anything to be kept in SHU, but who the administration had no intention of allowing on the mainline. There were program activities for prisoners there (yard, recreation, etc.), and the prison accomplished its primary purpose—to separate prisoners who were classified as such from mainline prisoners.

Judge Henderson was wrong in his ruling that prison group membership affiliation justifies indeterminate terms. Many of the indeterminate termers are in SHU for non–disciplinary reasons. Many were in general population for months or years [while] identified and classified as prison group members. Judge Henderson's ruling simply does not take those prisoners into consideration. Any corrective strategy will have to start by committing ourselves to reducating people, out of, and away from, the perception that has been created about prisoners in SHU. It is easy to justify subjecting prisoners to this kind of madness when they are defined as "the worst of the worst" instead of as human beings. Perhaps even Judge Henderson's ruling was influenced by this. None of the cats were considered to be "gang members" fifteen to twenty years ago. When you consider the perception most people have about gangs (the cause for peoples' fear and one of the major cause of many of the social problems in society), it is easy to see how they can justify and receive support for the inhumanities they subject people to.

Sadly, the majority of people in this country only relate to what they can see, hear, feel, and touch. Any time the country is confronted with serious/important issues they usually opt for whatever is easiest. Rarely are people willing to have a discussion in an attempt to reach an understanding and to accomplish some meaningful lasting solution. [In this country, people are quick to criticize and condemn other countries for doing some of the same things to people that they support here.]

I think before any positive action can result from any strategy, first an effort must be made to re-educate people. Challenge them to start viewing and defining things for what they really are, and to stop relying on politicians to make the kinds of decisions that we should be making our/themselves. Encourage people to recognize and understand how they are influenced to think in such a way that they constantly support ideas that are clearly not in anyone's interest. The very

37

same problems and causes still exist today that existed thirty years ago. The only meaningful difference is that the problems are no longer considered to be only poor peoples' problems. A strategy that does not emphasize changing the way people think will be ineffective.

I must also emphasize that if the next generation is to have a chance at not being subjected to this kind of madness, those of us who righteously care have the responsibility to make them aware of what this reality is, that it is not necessary to come to places like this to learn to develop into men. The fact that many of these young people, particularly those of color, are already imprisoned and keep coming back is at least some proof that they are not being schooled on how to stay out of these places. They continue to make many of the same mistakes that we did and because they do, their children will probably make the same mistakes. At some point, some of us will have to say the young deserve better than this and will have to begin to teach them what they have to know to effectively build, create, change, and win!

Judge Henderson's ruling in the other areas was timely, and courageous, and will help particular prisoners in need of help. The fact that litigation was/is necessary to determine how people should not treat other people speaks volumes about just how uncivilized many have become in this country. But I think the inconsistency in the ruling is typical of the hypocrisy in this country.

The ruling leaves in place the "debrief, parole, or die in SHU" policy for indeterminate prisoners, but it established that the act of debriefing/informing can lead to not only to the prisoner who does this being hurt or killed, but also that prisoner's family and loved ones. Judge Henderson's ruling, in this respect, suggests that this is simply a consequence we must accept, in order to maintain the appearance of security. I (like many other indeterminate termers) have been back here for more than

38

five years now, and I have been isolated, had my mail checked, and rechecked, etc., and no one can tell tell them anything they have not already been told years ago, or that they have not already learned themselves. If it is true there are approximately 600 prisoners in SHU serving an indeterminate term, then the majority of prisoners classified as "gang members" are in the general population, not in SHU. So this policy is, in reality, only directed toward certain people and part of the reason for the Judge's ruling was to check the abuses that were occurring. There is absolutely no reason for anyone to believe these people will not continue to abuse this policy. I, and others, have been told by the CSR represen-tative in Sacramento that retaining people in SHU and releasing people from SHU on indeterminate terms is done on a case–by–case basis. [This has nothing to do withdebriefing.]

But more than anything, it is not necessary to house prisoners in Pelican Bay SHU exclusively, because there are other SHUs in the California Department of Corrections that can accomplish the same thing. Contrary to what has been said, one SHU is no different than the next, in terms of what it intends to accomplish—to separate certain prisoners from the mainline and to maintain security.

The only way they can justify warehousing certain prisoners is by taking the position that this SHU is the only one that houses indeterminate termers. Judge Henderson's ruling did not go far enough in dealing with this, and it should have, particularly when you consider the Judge, himself, acknowledged the psychological effects of being back here for a long period of time. We have to keep these contradictions out there and have them judged or questioned.

MICHAEL DORROUGH
D-83611

THE SAME OLD GAME

Once again prisoners have been used as tools or pawns to justify ills of society. Like in any other circus where animals are paraded in front of audiences for entertainment, greed, unscrupulous motives or stupidity . . . the prisoners were made to believe we would benefit or receive justice in the Madrid Case. What we got was another blow of reality—we will continue to be used by politicians, courts, lawyers and self-serving organizations to further their interests while we continue to suffer from the most inhumane conditions possible in a so-called "civilized" society. It was obvious with all the "Get Tough on Crime, Build More Prisons, Punish the Prisoners, etc." hoopla that nothing was going to benefit us prisoners in SHU with the present atmosphere and mentality of society and the media propaganda creating such a scare, how were prisoners in Pelican Bay SHU going to receive anything? What purpose the lawsuit served was not to our benefit, in fact, all the media attention probably did more harm by securing the negative attitudes of people in society that we in SHU or in prison generally are getting what we deserve.

What good did Judge Henderson's ruling do? If I lie and call it a partial victory, I may as well cease struggling and place my trust in those seeking to exploit us. Myself and the approximate 50% of prisoners in SHU serving indeterminate SHU terms didn't get anything except another slap. We are the ones subjected to the repressive, isolated and torturous conditions described in the lawsuit. We are the ones experiencing long-term solitary confinement and at risk of developing harmful psychological conditions. Those who were supposed to benefit didn't, so what are we supposed to be excited about, being sacrificed for better medical or psychiatric care? That's a mirage, an illusion. The medical care is as is, the psychiatric care was resolved in the *Coleman* case but neither of these rulings has substance if you're a prisoner in the SHU everyday. I don't think anyone here was foolish enough to believe the SHU would be shut down. . . .

The State doesn't spend hundreds of millions of dollars on torture chambers to shut them down. Every part of the system knows its functions and the courts' functions are to rule in favor of the State when society's castaways are the sacrificial lambs. What I worry about is how those who supposedly represent us mislead us by building our hopes and then selling us out. What these opportunists who claim to represent us should do is use some of the millions paid in court fees and contributions to educate the masses in society about what is really behind the prison expansion nationwide and the control units, to urge the people to unite and protest this racist political line being pushed by self-serving, rightwing politicians and demagogues. Don't become pawns yourself, get with us or leave us alone.

GEORGE MOSLEY
C-33118

Every
Pelican Bay inmate
is familiar with
the cruelty of housing
mentally ill inmates,
known as "J-cats,"
in close proximity
to inmates who,
according to the institution,
are sympathizers or
known gang members.
This facility
has not provided
the range of mental services
needed here in the Security
Housing Unit.
They believe
locking up an individual
solves any problem,
even mental disease.
The only people who suffer
are the J-cats
and inmates
wrongly labelled
by CDC as gang members.
The stench,
the screaming don't stop.
It only echoes
through these walls.
Hence, all inmates
are anomie
in their own sense. . . !

BENIGNO OCHOA
H-35089

ON DEBRIEFING

(A) The California Department of Correction's Debriefing Program is an underground policy which affects only a relative handful of prisoners, leaving the great majority free, for the time being, from the debriefing re-straint.

(B) A survey of Title 15 of the Director's Rule indicates that the vast majority of rules and regulations designated cover every act of misbehavior. The California Prison Authority uses the existence of ongoing conspiracy to create the appearance of danger to institutional security. This enables the Prison Authority to punish disfavored prisoners for infractions that break no rules.

(C) Once an informant identifies a prisoner as a member and/or associate of a prison gang in California, a rigid rule of debriefing is applied inflexibly without regard to the unique circumstances of each case.

(D) No prisoner could conceive that it is not within the power of the Prison Authority to prohibit acts intended to disrupt the security of the institution. The question we are concerned with is whether the Prison Authority has the power to impose debriefing on a disfavored group of prisoners, under the cover of institutional security. Prison Authority, through its classification committee, implies Title 15 Director Rules do not apply when it comes to any prisoner identified with a prison gang. The California Prison Authority says through its actions that an ongoing conspiracy by prison gangs justifies the debriefing program. Accepting this, and allowing it to go unchallenged, validates this unconstitutional procedure.

(E) The debriefing program's real design is not only to eradicate so-called prison gangs, but also to create a pool of informants and to regulate conduct within its boundaries.

This part of an experimentation program will eventually be applied to all groups of prisoners regardless of social, religious, or political association. The State Prison Authority wants to first regulate the personal activities of the prisoner class throughout the country and the civilian population of free society. The end result will be fascism.

1. Question: *Lieutenant Z, where are you employed and in what capacity?* Answer: I presently work for the CDC, the California Department of Corrections, at Pelican Bay State Prison as an I.G.I. (Institutional Gang Investigator).

2. Q: *What training and experience qualifies you as an I.G.I.?* A: Extensive experience dealing with prison gangs, and particular training identifying, detecting, investigating, and prosecuting prison gang activities. I've attended numerous seminars and training conferences on prison gangs, and have a background in identifying various prison gang activities and modes of operation within and without the prison system.

3. Q: *What does an I.G.I. do?* A: Gathers and maintains information regarding prison gangs and gang activities at Pelican Bay, and conducts debriefings of those inmates who wish to disassociate themselves.

4. Q: *Now direct your attention to Exhibit A, debriefing report in the name of _____ , Record Number ____ . Are you acquainted with those particular records, and have you viewed them before?* A: Yes, this Number ___ is the number given to the particular subject, Inmate A.

5. Q: *Can you tell us if you ever conducted a debriefing of Inmate A?* A: Yes, on _____ .

6. Q: *Can you tell us when you first came into contact with Inmate A, and under what circumstances?* A: I received an interview request slip from inmate A's unit counselor, stating he requested to be interviewed for debriefing. I had the escorting officer bring him to the IGI office under pretense that the sergeant wanted to see him.

7. Q: *Approximately how many IGI officers were involved in the debriefing?* A: Two other lieutenants were involved.

8. Q: *How is the debriefing report classified?* A: Confidential.

9. Q: *Does an inmate undergoing debriefing waive his Fifth Amendment right of self-incrimination?* A: The inmate is not forced to incriminate himself in violation of the Fifth Amendment. He may raise the issue of his rights being violated should those statements be introduced in a subsequent prosecution. As a policy, the CDC does not prosecute or discipline inmates based on information obtained during debriefing.

10. Q: *Why would an inmate undergo debriefing and be stigmatized as an informant?* A: The inmate will benefit in several ways, plus it shows his sincerity in disassociating himself from the gang in order for the gang classification to be removed from his central file.

11. Q: *Does the inmate always tell everything he knows, including the role he played in criminal activities as a gang member?* A: Initially, no. The interviewers expect the subject to conceal certain offenses from the debriefing. It is felt that most subjects will be apprehensive at first.

12. Q: *Was Inmate A initially apprehensive?* A: Inmate A was not apprehensive at all. He fully cooperated with the interviewers.

13. Q: *And what makes Inmate A different from others who showed some apprehension?* A: Well, Inmate A has provided the Department of Correction (CDC) with reliable information many times in the past. Prior to coming to prison, he had provided local police with information during a criminal investigation.

14. Q: *So the stigma of being an informant does not hinder Inmate A?* A: No, in fact, he believes it's a necessary step towards rehabilitation and becoming a productive citizen in society.

15. Q: *Lt. Z, have you ever done any intelligence work outside of the CDC?* A: Prior to working for the CDC, I was involved with military intelligence while in the Navy.

16. Q: *Are you still working as an agent for military intelligence today?* A: No, I am not.

17. Q: *Prior to _____, were you aware of Inmate A providing the CDC with reliable information?* A: Yes, I was aware that he had provided information in the past.

18. Q: *Did Inmate A ever provide you with information prior to _____?* A: No.

19. Q: *What does the term "reliable information" mean?* A: Information which the informant witnessed himself, or which the criminal, himself, told to the informant.

20. Q: *How do you determine if information is accurate and not deceptive?* A: If the inmate tells us what another classified relevant informant has told us, this is one means of determining accuracy, or if he tells about more recent offenses of the same type, or if he told us about more serious offenses. Those inmates who are categorized as "deceptive/questionable" told us about offenses which were similar to, but did not exactly match, offenses about which the State already had information.

21. Q: *How do you determine whether or not information is exaggerated?* A: Well, to safeguard against exaggeration, we have a set of detailed questions we ask.

22. Q: *How did you come to know Inmate A as an informant?* A: Another inmate gave Inmate A's name during debriefing as an active member of the _____ prison gang, along with other names.

23. Q: *The inmate who gave Inmate A's name during debriefing, did he complete a successful debriefing?* A: Yes, he did.

24. Q: *Did Inmate B's information about Inmate A prove reliable?* A: Yes.

25. Q: *Lt. Z, from whom did you learn Inmate B was an informant?* A: After learning about Inmate B's membership in the _____ gang, I ran his name through the computer and had his central file brought over to the IGI office. After reviewing his file, I learned about the information he had provided to CDC in the past.

26. Q: *Did you learn during your debriefing of Inmate B that he had, himself, been involved in some criminal activity?* A: Yes, the mere fact that extensive confidential information exists indicating Inmate B's membership in the ___ prison gang is evidence of criminal activity involvement.

27. Q: *Lt. Z, did you learn that Inmate A was directly involved in the murder of another inmate?* A: Yes, during the debriefing of Inmate B, we learned of Inmate A's alleged involvement in the death of an inmate.

28. Q: *The information about A's involvement in a homicide, did the IGI determine it to be reliable?* A: We determined that Inmate A may have knowledge surrounding the death of an inmate.

29. Q: *Was criminal prosecution sought against Inmate A?* A: No.

30. Q: *Was Inmate A issued a CDC 115?* A: No.

31. Q: *Was Inmate A given immunity from prosecution during his debriefing if he provided information regarding the murder he allegedly participated in?* A: No immunity was given or offered to Inmate A.

32. Q: *Did Inmate A tell you about his role in the murder?* A: No, he did not.

33. Q: *To your knowledge, did you or any other IGI question Inmate A about the murder during his debriefing?* A: No, we did not.

34. Q: *Is there some reason why Inmate A was not debriefed on the murder he is alleged to have participated in over a decade ago?* A: The IGI interviewers know concealment varies from one inmate to another, and certain offenses of a statute of limitation will be concealed more often than other offenses without one. If the inmate undergoes debriefing, is questioned about his role in a homicide, and does not provide us with detailed information, he will feel that no real reward will be forthcoming, so why debrief? The debriefing procedure is based on the strategy of convincing the inmate he will benefit. He would not provide information if he felt he would be prosecuted in court.

35. Q: *Let me understand clearly, an inmate can escape prosecution for a murder by just debriefing and providing reliable information on others?* A: Absolutely not.

36. Q: *Well, has any inmate who has successfully debriefed ever been prosecuted for any criminal activity still within the statute of limitations?* A: No, not to my knowledge.

37. Q: *To your knowledge, is there a statute of limitation for murder?* A: No, there is not.

38. Q: *Does the IGI have the option of prosecuting those debriefers who commit a criminal offense at a later date?* A: That is not our job, it is up to the State Attorney General's Office if prosecution is sought at a later date.

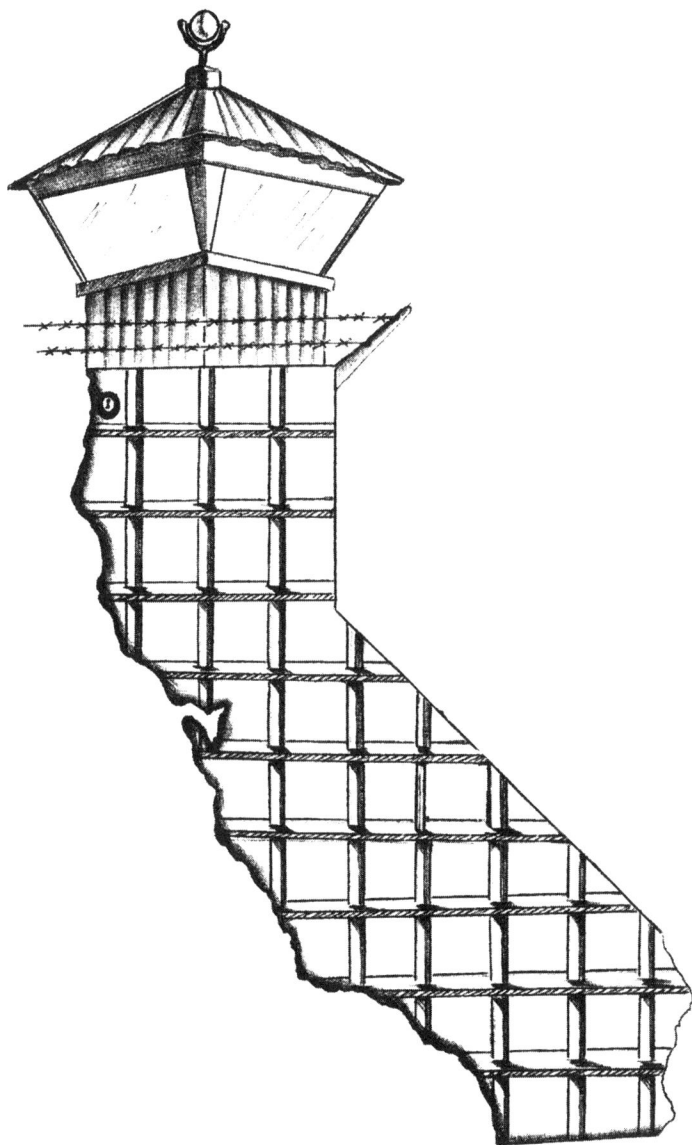

BRAULIO CASTELLANOS
C-15703

49

39. Q: *What is the first thing you ask when an inmate is before the IGI debriefing?* A: An inmate debriefing before us has completed the first pre-debriefing examination by providing us with a handwritten biography account of how he came to be involved with the gang and recruitment requirements. The IGI interviewers are selectively chosen to gain the confidence of the inmate. We explain the debriefing process. We then ask the inmate to help us by supplying names of every member of the gang, as well as those in close association to the gang. After this, we ask him who he knows that has committed criminal acts for which they have not been caught, together with as much as he can tell us about the criminal act he has revealed. The interviewers assure the debriefer of confidentiality and anonymity, and we stress the importance of truthfulness in a successful debriefing.

40. Q: *Does secondhand information count as reliable?* A: If other sources have provided the same information, or if the inmate has proven reliable after successfully undergoing debriefing, then, yes, secondhand information is reliable, within the framework of the institutional order.

41. Q: *Do you tape record and/or video tape debriefings?* A: All debriefing interviews are [now] recorded for voice identification, as well as video taped.

42. Q: *What about polygraph examination, does everyone who debriefs take one?* A: No, in part, and yes, in part.

43. Q: *Please explain your answer.* A: Debriefing inmates who, themselves, have been involved in criminal activity that falls within the statute of limitation are not given polygraphs as a policy on the statute of limitation offenses. If we ask the inmate about his involvement in a murder and do not give him immunity, he will lie, and be

deceptive about his role. Therefore, the polygraph will show his untruthfulness. Plus, he does not know that we already have reliable information about his participation.

44. Q: *So if an inmate takes a polygraph and fails, would he still be deemed reliable on other information?* A: Not necessarily. The polygraph is just a tool.

45. Q: *Is that the reason Inmate A was not required to undergo polygraph examination about his alleged involvement in a murder?* A: No, the fact is that Inmate A has provided accurate information in the past, and has met the criteria by incriminating himself and others in illegal activities per section 312 of the classification manual and Title 15, Article 5, Section 3321, so we felt a polygraph was not warranted at that time.

46. Q: *What type of machine does your office use for polygraph examination of debriefing?* A: We use an ultra-scribe produced by Stolty, a multifunction instrument capable of making three different types of recordings required by law: respiration, skin response, and cardiovascular tracings.

47. Q: *Besides inmates not given polygraphs on criminal offenses that have no statute of limitation, are there any other inmates not required to take polygraphs?* A: Yes, inmates determined unsuitable for testing, such as schizophrenics. Some inmates are not psychologically suitable for tests. For example, inmates under the influence of certain drugs would be medically unsuitable.

48. Q: *Does Inmate A know that another inmate has provided confidential information about his involvement in criminal activities?* A: Yes, he does.

49. Q: *Does he know that information about his involvement in a murder has been provided?* A: I have no idea; neither I, nor any other IGI official have made reference to it.

50. Q: *What is the intent, purpose, and objective of this debriefing procedure?* A: To break the will of prison gangs and their membership. The procedure is based on the strategy that if at least half the criminal gangs debriefed, the interviewers would then have a pool of information on everyone. The intent is to create as many informants as possible within the prison population until half are informing on the other half.

51. Q: *Is the policy designed to have all inmates debriefing incriminate themselves in criminal activity?* A: Yes.

52. Q: *If an inmate does not incriminate himself, but tells you everything he knows about others' criminal activities, how will his debriefing be affected?* A: As a matter of policy, the inmate will be considered a concealer of information if he doesn't confess to an offense about which a previous informant has told us.

53. Q: *So, in essence, the debriefing procedure is based on the strategy that each inmate corroborates what another said about him during debriefing?* A: That is your interpretation.

54. Q: *And what is your interpretation?* A: The IGI policy holds that in order for an inmate to successfully debrief, he must make a showing of sincerity and good faith by asserting membership and/or association in a criminal prison gang he has claimed to be part of. Once the information he gives is classified as reliable, as a matter of policy we do not question it, and to this date, all prior confidential information has proven reliable. Classification remains the same until reliable information indicates otherwise, or until the inmates provide reliable contradictory information.

55. Q: *How does an inmate provide reliable information that he is not associated with a prison gang?* A: He does through the debriefing process.

56. Q: *Earlier you stated the debriefing procedure is built around convincing the inmate he will benefit in several ways. In which ways will the inmate benefit?* A: The gang classification is removed, and he can be moved to a less restricted environment. If the inmate is under a life term, he will be able to meet his parole suitability requirements of general population placement. The inmate can benefit through the visiting program, both contact and conjugal visits become available. He also becomes eligible to draw more canteen each month and to receive special purchases he could not make while in security housing.

57. Q: *Are inmates who debrief and/or move to less restrictive environments placed in the general prison population?* A: In most cases they will remain in the security housing unit (SHU) until they complete their SHU term. If they have no SHU term, they are usually transferred to another institution where they either go into general population or are placed in a management control unit (MCU) for a period.

58. Q: *Inmates placed in a MCU have no SHU term to complete?* A: That is correct.

59. Q: *Why do some inmates go straight into the general population, and others go into a MCU?* A: In some cases the IGI interviewers were not certain whether during the debriefing something was deliberately being concealed or distorted, or whether the memories of the informants merely differed about the same information. This is a security precaution in case an inmate has feigned disassociation and escaped our detection.

60. Q: *Once an inmate has made it to the* MCU, *how do you determine if he is feigning disassociation?* A: That inmate will go through a post-debriefing test as proof of sincerity and good faith because the safety of inmates and staff requires further evidence.

61. Q: *Please elaborate on the post-debriefing test.* A: Post-debriefing interviews last from thirty-five minutes to two hours for each session. There is a standard questionnaire of 50 questions. Each question describes something a fellow gang member might have done. The post-debriefing test is classified confidential. To elaborate any further would threaten the debriefing process.

62. Q: *Are inmates who are placed within the general prison population during the course of debriefing under any special conditions ?* A: You will have to be specific when you inquire about special conditions.

63. Q: *Is the inmate required to provide the CDoC with ongoing information about any illegal activities he witnesses in the future?* A: That depends. Inmates who undergo debriefing are instructed for their own safety to report on inmates who are involved in prison gang activity. Sometimes an inmate may spot someone who has strong association ties with a prison gang, and for his own safety he may report it to the IGI. We also encourage cooperation and communication between the inmate and staff.

64. Q: *Are ex-gang members used to control their respective ethnic groups within the general prison population?* A: As I understand you, no. It is against departmental rules to use inmates in a leadership role to control other inmates. I believe that is listed under Title 15, Section 3022.

65. Q: *Does the IGI recommend, or directly place an ex-gang member who has debriefed into the men's advisory*

committee (M.A.C.)? A: We may recommend the inmate get involved in noncriminal activities, such as Christian study groups, school curriculums, or M.A.C. This helps establish positive norms and role expectation for adult social life. It meets the need for group-fulfillment and allows ex-gang members to talk freely in front of, and to, correctional staff. This helps prepare the ex-gang member to meet parole eligibility requirements and responsibilities.

66. Q: *Is an inmate who debriefs considered a state informant who will give information from time to time?* A: If a serious incident occurs in the general area of the ex-gang member, we require him to answer truthfully any questions related to the incident, in order to protect him from being falsely accused.

67. Q: *What happens to the inmate considered a state informant who does not provide information pertaining to an incident he has first- or second-hand knowledge of?* A: During investigation he may be returned to the SHU until he has been cleared of any involvement.

68. Q: *Has any debriefer serving a life sentence received a parole date?* A: I have no idea, and that is not my concern.

69. Q: *Does anyone from the IGI office make favorable recommendations to the Board of Prison Terms (BPT)?* A: I have not, and no one, to my knowledge, ever has.

70. Q: *You stated earlier that your IGI office did not seek prosecution on discovering information pertaining to the homicide of an inmate. Was anyone else informed?* A: Yes, a CDoC Form _____ packet was completed per procedure. One copy was sent to the Special Service Unit (SSU), and another was sent to the State Attorney General's Special Prosecution Section.

71. Q: *What is the purpose of videotaping debriefing sessions?* A: It is done in case prosecution is sought against another gang member and the inmate who has debriefed dies before he can testify. It also ensures against subjects (debriefers) who later recant information, denying it or claiming it was misinterpreted.

72. Q: *Do you release copies of videotaped debriefings to other law enforcement agencies?* A: Only when an agency requests it through the Great System Data Base.

73. Q: *Lt. Z, what is the "containment theory?"* A: Isolation for gang members away from the gang structure, which leaves many of them vulnerable, and unable to function alone.

74. Q: *Is this part of the strategy to induce debriefing?* A: Yes, the objective of debriefing includes destroying a subject's gang identification.

75. Q: *Does the IGI operate outside the prison facility?* A: Only within the Department of Corrections' framework of the SSU.

76. Q: *Are inmates who have debriefed and paroled back to the outside required to provide the Department of Correction's SSU with on-going information about any illegal activities on the part of other parolees?* A: If a subject is questioned by his parole officer, or any law enforcement agency about any criminal investigation pertaining to another parolee in his general area, then, yes, he is required to answer truthfully about any first, or secondhand information he may have. This also protects him from being falsely suspected and/or accused. Any information he provides can also serve to shorten his parole period.

77. Q: *What if he refuses to provide information that he may, or may not, have?* A: He could be charged with obstruction of justice and have his parole revoked.

78. Q: *Is an inmate who has debriefed required to give testimony if a Grand Jury is convened against any of the prison gangs?* A: I would think anyone subpoenaed before a Grand Jury would be obligated to answer questions put to them.

79. Q: *Are prison gang members required to debrief before being released from an indeterminate SHU sentence, and if so, what are the names of those prison gangs?* A: Yes, they are. There is the ___, and the _____, and _____. Also the _____.

80. Q: *Does an official debriefing policy exist?* A: Yes.

81. Q: *Is this an underground policy?* A: No, it's confidential in nature.

82. Q: *Is the debriefing policy derived from some form of military procedure?* A: Yes, it is.

83. Q: *Are all prison gangs considered criminal gangs?* A: Yes, they are.

Submitted by
NEW AFRIKAN PRISONERS
INSIDE THE SECURITY HOUSING UNIT
PELICAN BAY STATE PRISON
CRESCENT CITY, CALIFORNIA

SECTION III. BEYOND THE GLASS

. . . .When history appears to be static, it is the oppressed who are shut out. History is not only closed, but specifically closed against them. The past is forgotten, the future is foreclosed, and there is only the never-ending present to be endured. The poor are told this is the way things have always been and forever will be. What cannot be allowed to be believed or imagined is the possibility of hope for a new day.

. . . . Changes, possiblities, opportunities, and surprises no one or very few would even have imagined become history after they've occurred. . . . In each case, the gains, victories, and transformations seemed impossible at first and became possible only by stepping through the door of hope. Spiritual visionaries have often been the first to walk through that door, because in order to walk through it, first you have to see it, and then you have to believe that something lies on the other side. . . .Those who walk through the door must also be prepared to suffer and even to die, because the door of hope always leads from one reality to another. . . . It's never easy, never without pain or suffering. And it's always hardest for the first few who take those steps.

JIM WALLIS, *THE SOUL OF POLITICS: A PRACTICAL AND PROPHETIC VISION FOR SOCIAL CHANGE (THE NEW PRESS AND ORBIS BOOKS, 1994).*

INTRA-REVOLUTIONARY INITIATIVE

"The law is the last resort of human wisdom acting upon human experience for the benefit of the public." — *Samuel Johnson*

The basic foundations upon which this Nation rest have inherent flaws that fracture the organic concept drafted by the Founding Fathers over two hundred years ago. Approximately one hundred years later, during the period in our history known as the "Reconstruction," these inborn flaws were brought to light. From those early days up to today and pressing on beyond tomorrow, those faulty characteristics will never—by themselves—change. These perpetual errors will continue until people recognize the problems incorporated into the concept which governs their lives. The Constitution of the United States was drafted by elitists on behalf of a class or race of people. It did not include all people, as it is interpreted today, although that should have been the initial intent.

Native Americans, slave negroes, and other indigenous peoples of the time were not included. The Constitution affirmed the imbalance that persists to this day. It should be noted that during the "Reconstruction," Congress intended to afford negro minorities the same rights as whites had been accorded from the beginning. However, this attempt, no matter how perceived, only further deepened the flaws inherent in the Constitution because it brought the issue of race to light, acknowledged disparities, *but* affirmed the differences by making a futile attempt to correct them. This is one reason why during the sixties, the grassroots movement of people such as Martin Luther King, Jr. floundered while seeking civil rights. These problems continue to plague us even today because the basic foundations upon which this Nation rests are imperfect and unchanging.

The Constitution of the United States sets forth fundamental legal rights. It limits the powers of government and protects individual liberties. The Constitution is an expression of the people's will to be governed and serves, in effect, as a "natural law" for the United States. The idea of natural law was based on English jurisprudence which believed that laws of nature should govern human affairs. This natural law theory was based, in part, on the observation that nature imposed an order on all forms of life. Therefore, the laws governing human affairs should promote the order as Nature had provided. In addition, natural law theory fit prevailing religious beliefs. Religious scholars taught that God controlled the natural order of the world and gave humans the ability to reason between right and wrong. Therefore, man was accountable to God for maintaining the order that God had given to the world.

Our law, both philosophically and structurally, is supposed to evolve constantly in response to changes in America. As a means of social control, it is supposed to reflect—gradually—society's changing values.

When the Constitution was drafted, its preamble declared in bold letters "We The People," referring to all people of the new union calling itself the "United States of America." It held the following truths to be self-evident: that all men were created equal and were endowed by God Almighty with certain unalienable rights which consist in part of life, liberty, and the pursuit of happiness.

When the United States' Constitution became the Supreme law of the land, it set into motion what should have been profound changes that abolished inequality, slavery, racism, and poverty at the time of enactment. Yet as we know, it did not. Why? Because the Constitution leaves power in the hands of a few elitists who circumvent and manipulate the system for selfish gain. Although based on the theory of natural law, the document was drafted at a time when indigenous people were not recognized, and viewed as inferior.

Thus, today the people must impel the transition to change the flaws of the past for a more secure future. This they must do either through full scale revolution, civil unrest, or by invoking

MARCOS EDUARDO VIGIL
C-36354

63

the full force and effect of their rights. And it is inevitable that change within this society and government must occur. The Declaration of Independence provides some guidance where it proclaims:

> "Whenever any form of government becomes destructive of these ends (life, liberty, happiness, inter-alia), it is the right of the people to alter or abolish it, and to institute new government . . ."

An Intra-Revolutionary Initiative is required to "alter" or "abolish" the Constitution (in part) and to institute major and profound changes that would repair the currently inherent flaws, and to include clauses of stipulations put in place to prevent government abuses, and sanctions for government representatives found to manipulate or circumvent the trust of the people, for their own agendas, so as to provide for the general welfare of all its people, and to abolish inequality, racism and poverty.

Such an initiative would be set forth by the people through petition and would call for the people themselves to elect who shall attend. They would decide the agenda, the issues to be discussed regarding changes that must be made to correct flaws in the constitution, and what is required to fix them, the ultimate vote would be through the people themselves, all people within in the borders or territories of the United States, and final approval would come by their vote.

Such an "initiative" would take time, possibly years, yet it is the only way to correct flaws that have existed for over two hundred years, and to provide a future that secures the blessings of life, liberty, and the pursuit of happiness for all people within the United States of America, both now, and for generations as yet to come.

FREDDY MEDINA
C-16571

What type of prisoner does our society wish to encounter and deal with upon eventual parole? With about a million and a half men and women in prisons and jails in this country, [this] question becomes larger and more important every day. Prison reform is not an issue only for prisoners; it should be a concern for all citizens who care about living in a just and safe society. A few essentials that should be demanded for prison reform are:

1. Mandatory educational job training programs for all prisoners;

2. Community resources (in and out of prison) to enable the prisoner to stay in contact with the community, giving the prisoner the chance to understand how his or her destructive acts have hurt the community. The goal should be to allow the prisoner to spend his or her time behind bars figuring out how best to utilize this time to rectify past destructive acts and make the transition to being a constructive member of society;

3. Independent investigation and monitoring of prison officials' conduct;

4. Mechanisms of accountability so prison officials cannot hide behind their claim of "qualified immunity" for acts of brutality;

5. Prison lobby and support groups, so prisoners have place to turn for help.

These reforms would at least give prisoners a way to have a positive impact on the institution. Citizens must stop allowing themselves to be duped into believing those classified as the "criminal element" are the cause of all of society's ills, and begin to deal with the real causes of unemployment, homeless, etc. Only then will we be able to create a society that is safe and beneficial for all its citizens, and not just the select few.

C. ASKARI KWELI
S/N FLOYD NELSON
B-94350

■ ■ ■ ■ ■

BEHIND THE GLASS

Knock! Knock! Knock! Wake up! who's there? Time for Action!!! Listen here, we are faced with a very sad tragedy that requires immediate focus: SOLUTIONS WITHIN OUR REACH & CONTROL! We as a people/minority within the communities and behind prison walls have within our reach the power to bring an end to the corrupt injustice system manipulating the infliction that is destroying us at a rapid pace through divisions.

The first phase of the solution is very simple and clear— it's called "UNITY"–coming together to work together, and the oppressor–the administration, etc.—is no match for that kind of power. George Jackson said it in a loud, clear tone. I quote : "Can you see the division among us? and its effect? This is our greatest obstacle. I sometimes wonder how this will turn out. Before we can ever effectively face down the foe, we must have had long since learned to share, trust, communicate and live harmoniously with each other."

George Jackson said this in 1971 and see the effect in 1995 in our communities and prisons. Mass unity can give us the power to organize and cripple the administration throughout California prisons on a massive level that will strip them of this abusive power they are enjoying with a passion. Our unity will serve and benefit us and allow us to have a direct link to our communities to work within, creating a positive productive image to generate a new wave of community support. A first step to implementing a solution as Jonathan Jackson once said: "Talking has ended—action has begun!" I will depart with words from Freidrich Nietzsche: "Distrust all in whom the impulse to punish is powerful."

In Unity,

BROTHER PAUL REDD
B-72683

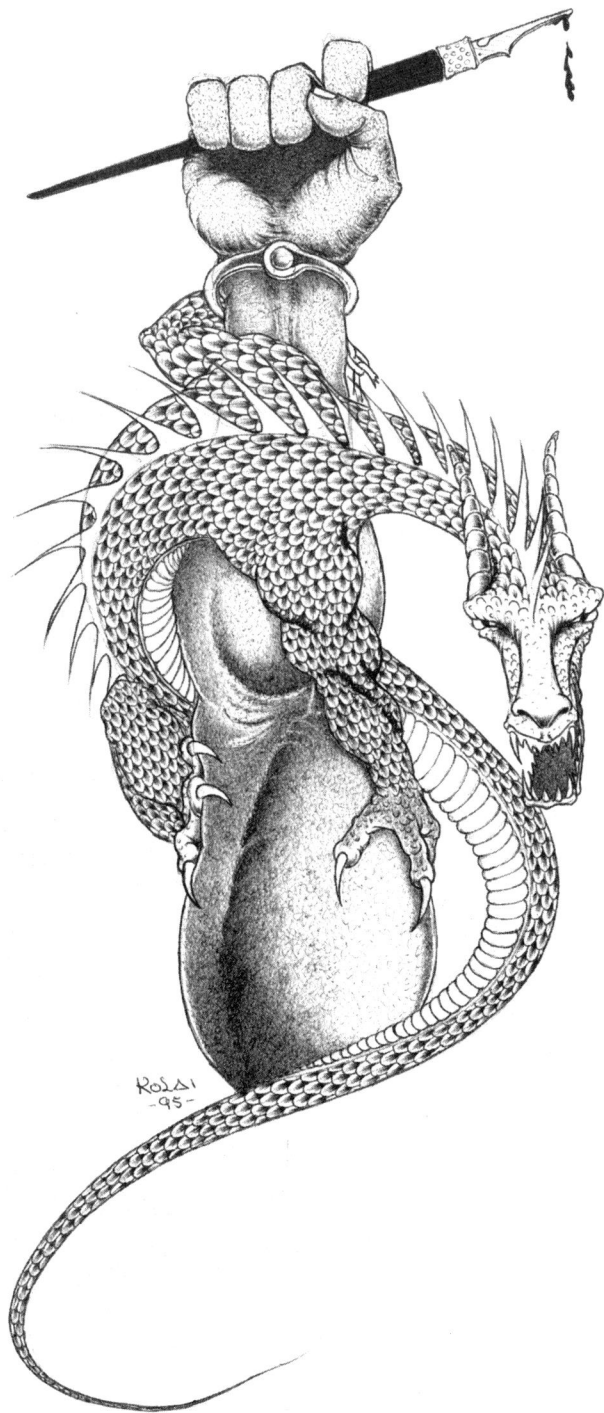

EDUCATION AS A STRATEGY

Eurocrats know and understand the fact that there is power in the control of knowledge. This is the reason they do not wish many people to succeed socially and economically. They make sure the oppressed do not become conscious, they place obstacles and refractions in the way to detour them from becoming conscious of the truth about "knowledge" and its power.

This is why it is very important for us to seek to educate ourselves. RAZA! We need to learn about our own history, the Aztecas, Zapata, Villa, Los Zoot-Suiters and the 60s and 70s movement. There is a long line of our Raza's history we could learn from. Most importantly, we must come to understand the extreme importance of studying the struggles of our RAZA against assimilation, so we can apply our most effective defense strategies to our own struggle for prison reform, self-education, self-rehabilitation and liberation, from these Eurocrats.

The time has arrived for each of us prisoners to believe in ourselves and in our abilities. Seek the education necessary to open the eyes of your brothers and sisters, family and friends, to hold one another up in a positive war for reform. However, this task can only be accomplished through education. So take it upon yourselves to educate yourselves, so that you may be included in the driving force, educating those who will follow in your footsteps.

RUBEN L. CASTRELLON
E-27138

FREEDOM IS A STATE OF MIND

My predicament, they call it doing time,
has opened my eyes to see
the many things I took for granted in life
and realizing my true necessities.

So I try implementing self-discipline for control,
soul-searching, to see and change faults I hold inside,
accepting the things I cannot change,
all to gain a content piece of mind.

Also being thankful for what I've got,
accepting responsibility,
looking forward, to trying to make the best of each day,
not allowing my time to do me.

For freedom is but a state of mind,
for people on the outside commit suicide everyday.
Plus I know what I have committed to my mind
is one thing which cannot be taken away.

So if we realize all things come and go
and adapt our attitudes
toward an impartial optimistic mind,
we realize, things are not so bad
and we are all really doing time.
It all depends on you and what you make out of it.

ANONYMOUS
SHU PRISONER

■ ■ ■ ■ ■

EDUCATION IN PLACE OF IMPRISONMENT

The act of incarceration is a response to the failure of the educational system.

When education was truly a goal, the "learn or fail" system was in place. Reading, writing, and arithmetic were musts. One could not advance without completing required assignments. This policy is no longer enforced. Schools routinely produce functional illiterates. Classes have become battlegrounds, instead of learning environments. When teachers were paid adequately, a personal sense of contribution prevailed. Taxes were used to employ graduating students, and recirculated back into the educational system, resulting in advancements in technology and more jobs. Education gave people a sense of self; the feeling that they possessed the ability—via education—to hope, and the vision to realize possibilities.

In the mid 70s, when dollars were diverted from technology, education, and community development, generations lost the ability to see the future. Technology was coopted by private industry, social development became a term reserved for the poor, and education was sold to the highest income racket.

A new industry was invented—Corrections. The State of California now specializes in warehousing (holding human beings) instead of in prevention or rehabilitation! Between 1983 and 1993, the number of sentenced prisoners grew by 77,548 (a 203.9% increase). California had the largest prison population at the end of 1993 (Bureau of Justice Statistics) and more than 28 prisons in place. The Billion Dollar Question has to be: "At what cost to the economic fabric of California?"

The earlier an individual is educated about a potential problem, the sooner he or she learns how to dismiss assumptions, overcome difficulties, and find a solution. So education can prevent a given problem from escalating.

Prison was originally designed as a place where social deviants could be sent to practice penitence. In essence, it was a form of spiritual self restitution, an unlikely goal in a prison setting today, if not simply impossible.

Prison is now a place to which a person is sent merely because society has no idea how to help those who have become social deviants, nor does it wish to accept such responsibility.

The prison system is no more than a revolving door of citizens, with inevitable economic failure. The incarceration of 1.3 million inmates costs America $26.8 billion annually. This must result in rehabilitation of individuals capable of functioning in a freer society, a society whose foundation is based on development and employment.

JACK MORRIS
C-06409

■ ■ ■ ■ ■

ON MEDIA MANIPULATION

We are inundated with visual images daily from all over the nation and world. At any given time one can witness a massacre from a market place in what once was Yugoslavia or mangled bodies floating downriver in Rwanda. We saw the assassination of a political candidate recently in Mexico, and we saw a rogue policeman in South Africa murder men on T.V. With this in mind, we need to ask ourselves: Are we as a whole desensitized? Does focusing on violence distort and harden our outlook? For example, in the Rodney King trial, the jury was shown the tape of the beating over and over in slow motion. The purpose was to desensitize the jury from the savagery of the beating. The ulterior motive was to give a logical method to the madness in favor of the LAPD. It worked. This is the flip side to desensitization. One can become fatigued into compliance.

So are our opinions based on true information? Or are we manipulated into supporting a larger agenda? The pop-media dictates the information that we are fed. It runs in cycles that are injected into our minds in predictable ways. For instance, all the recent fury over child molestation was dictated by the media, via Oprah, Roseanne, and the McMartin case (which turned out in question). The U.S. became saturated with child abuse scenarios which had a cumulative effect and reached its apex in the recent kidnap/ murder in Northern California. Then there was the tabloid case of Michael Jackson.

What has become obscured in all of the posturing involved is that most cases of child molestation occur in the home by family members or friends. Around one half of all murders are committed by the same. Not all or even most convicts are child molesters (it's not an acceptable ideology in prison), and most murders happen in one's peer group (i.e., drug addicts on same, etc.). This is not to rationalize. This is to clarify. All crime is counterproductive and wrong. The point being: society has been fatigued into compliance via distorted images of the most horrifying kind (i.e., abuse of children). This has dictated a slot machine reaction of voters, passing paternalistic legislation dictated by soundbites and propaganda. Politicos are cashing in on the herd mentality. Do these politicians even have the ability to deal with the 14% unemployment rate in California? Do they have a vision to solve the recession? Do they have the ability to address real issues or can they only demagogue about crime and immigration?

All of this is dictated by images of horror and violence. Your deepest drives are being played upon by spin doctors. Sex and death are the deepest drives of the human mind. So has our vision of what's really going on been obscured? I think so. Our outlook has been tainted by propaganda and demagogues.

It's time to rethink.

DONALD JOHNSON
B95524

FRANK FERNANDEZ
D-61222

ON PREJUDICE

Recently some Red brothers within the prison system instituted a new policy for acceptance into the Native American Indian Religious-Spiritual Group. They want to require any prisoner who wishes to take part in the group's spiritual functions to produce a government roll number as proof of his Native American Indian ancestry. Interestingly enough, this was first put forth by the prison officials and has since been adopted as the Red brothers' position [those who have roll numbers]. This has reduced the group's size to but a handful. The implementation of such ignorance by Red brothers with roll numbers has deprived and denied various other Red brothers their spiritual ways, such as to sweat or to smoke the pipe (the most basic and important ceremonies).

Not all persons of "Red" ancestry have government roll numbers, and not all such person want one, yet they still practice their traditional spiritual ways. Who are these brothers to require a government roll number from other prisoners of Red (or Mestizo) ancestry? They should instead be inquiring and pursuing the prison's failure and obvious refusals to hire and employ a Spiritual Leader as mandated by the CDC Directors' Manual, or the failure until recently of the prison religious Director to purchase firewood with the State Budget allotment designated for such purposes.

Apparently we not only have to fight against government oppression of our traditional spiritual ways, but also against ourselves, and against those who have become agent-provocateurs, or puppets of the system. A roll number is nothing more than a tag of subjugation and capitulation.

LUIS V. RODRIGUEZ
C-33000

WHAT IS PEACE?

peace isn't hate   I thought you knew
Don't tell me I'm wrong I been black too long
Fighting a senseless fight   for senseless causes
To achieve a senseless goal since the day I was born
Watching my brothers and sisters die for senseless reasons.

peace isn't violence Don't get mad at me,
you know you started it all
I'm not your political puppet . Don't want to play
your game of ball.   "Army," you say, "Be all you can be."
Yeah, right!   In your world I can't even be me
cause I'll never be free.

peace isn't hypocritical.   I can plainly see
your world peace is hypocrisy
A thirteen-year- old kills another for your dollar bills,
and you say he's wrong. A nation's leader
kills thousands for barrels of oil,
and you say he's right.   Don't give me that hype!

peace isn't blind   So leave me alone
I been without too long I've always had less:
Job-less Dollar-less Home-less Father-less
Now you threaten my blackness. Attempt to take my
dignity. But you say it's true that world peace is you.
Then why am I so Black and Blue!

MAURICE KING
C-83898

■ ■ ■ ■ ■

NORTH/SOUTH PEACE PROCESS

All parties involved intend to establish peace with the confines of Pelican Bay State Prison through communication and mutual consent. This desired outcome will be accomplished with noncommittal assistance by the administrators and concerned staff of the Department of Corrections.

The process will commence through open line communication with inmate mediators acting as liaisons for the inmate population and the administrators effecting the desired outcome. The intermediaries in this endeavor have elected to accept this position and are, in fact, encouraged to do so by those they represent, specifically the groups labelled Southern and Northern Mexicans.

1. OBLIGATIONS OF INMATE PARTIES:

    A. All parties commit to on-going communication.
    B. All parties agree to end conflict via mediation.
    C. Inmate parties will acknowledge that a bonafide peace process is being established.
    D. All parties assume a shared responsibility to effect the obligations listed above.

2. OBLIGATIONS OF PRISON OFFICIALS:

    A. Prison administrators will make an honest effort to facilitate the peace process.
    B. Prison officials will utilize a method of clearing up confusion or rumor. Mediators and/or liaisons representing both groups will be brought into a SHU (Security Housing Unit) pod (or other alternative place) to initiate communication and dialogue.
    C. Release of inmates in the SHU to the general prison population will be considered by staff after a specified period of clean conduct in an integrated setting.

D. Max 'A' inmates serving SHU indeterminate terms will be considered eventually for lesser custody status.

E. The administration will give all SHU inmates the opportunity to earn one-for-one time credits through positive behavior.

3. EXPECTED ACCOMPLISHMENTS:

A. Total elimination of alleged gang confrontation(s).

B. Total elimination of North/South confrontation.

C. Fewer inmate–on–staff assaults.

D. Fewer inmate–on–inmate assaults.

E. Uninterrupted academic and educational access.

F. An over-all smoother running institution, with the possibility that this peace will spread to other prisons and areas.

4. FINANCIAL COMMUNITY IMPACT:

Impact on the State and surrounding communities will be extremely formidable, provided the above obligations, expectations, and accomplishments are met. To expand:

A. Legal matters and litigation, with its extensive, costly, and time-consuming process will be reduced at a substantial saving to the State.

B. The prison population will be reduced because of the decrease in the number of inmates serving time for crimes committed while incarcerated.

C. Family units will have the opportunity to establish community ties for re-entry into society with a greatly reduced rate of recidivism.

D. The financial cost of operating a maximum security institution is much higher than for a lesser security institution. Better atmosphere among inmates creates a safer, less stressful working environment for staff.

For these reasons and for benefits we will all share as the result of enforcing the above obligations, the inmates of the Security Housing Units in Pelican Bay State Prison reiterate that with the genuine concern(s) of administrators, we, the Northern and Southern Mexican inmate population, agree to accept terms of peace for the above stated results. Said peace to encompass the entire prison population once these concerns have been resolved.

RESPECTFULLY SUBMITTED 1/11/93,
3 PELICAN BAY SHU PRISONERS

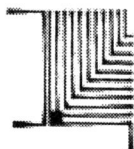

NO
MATTER
HOW LONG IT TAKES,
REAL CHANGES WILL COME,
AND THE GREATEST PERSONAL REWARD
LIES IN OUR INVOLVEMENT AND CONTRIBUTIONS,
EVEN IF IT MAY APPEAR THAT NOTHING SIGNIFICANT
OR OF IMPACT REALLY HAPPENED
DURING OUR TIMES.
BUT IT DID,
BECAUSE
EVERY SINCERE EFFORT
IS AS SPECIAL AS EVERY HUMAN LIFE.

HUGO PINELL
A-88401